Darkness Holding Light

Darkness Holding Light

Collection of Poems by Eugene Friends of Jung

Edited by
David H. Rosen
and
Carol Goodman

with illustrations by
Mary Willowmoon McDougal

RESOURCE *Publications* • Eugene, Oregon

DARKNESS HOLDING LIGHT
Collection of Poems by Eugene Friends of Jung

Copyright © 2016 Eugene Friends of Jung. All rights reserved. Except for brief quotations in critical publications or reviews, no part of this book may be reproduced in any manner without prior written permission from the publisher. Write: Permissions, Wipf and Stock Publishers, 199 W. 8th Ave., Suite 3, Eugene, OR 97401.

Sumi-e paintings © 2016 by Mary Willowmoon McDougal

Resource Publications
An Imprint of Wipf and Stock Publishers
199 W. 8th Ave., Suite 3
Eugene, OR 97401

www.wipfandstock.com

PAPERBACK ISBN: 978-1-4982-8200-0

Manufactured in the U.S.A. 3/10/2016

This book is dedicated to our dear friends and mentors:
Robin Jaqua & Sylvia Weisshaupt

Preface

This collection of poems is based on a Eugene Friends of Jung Seminar "Analytical Psychology and Poetry," led by David H. Rosen and held November 15, 2014 at the Wayne Morse Ranch in Eugene, Oregon. As Carl Jung maintained, poetry comes from the collective unconscious and this book reveals the truth of that statement. Poetry springs from the source, but is always reworked and refined by the ego, and in this case, feedback from seminar participants. The co-editor, Carol Goodman, was very helpful in obtaining poems from everyone and reviewing them.

David H. Rosen

Acknowledgments

We would like to thank all the members of Eugene Friends of Jung who contributed their Haiku and to Mary Willowmoon McDougal for the permission to use her original paintings. Our deepest gratitude to Dr. David H. Rosen for inspiring this collection of poetry.

In order of appearance:

Chris Piche, Chris White, Linda Sherman, Paul Helms, Karen Wickham, Dale O'Brien, Dean Schlect, Martha Binstadt, Mary Willowmoon McDougal, Avonelle Kluessendorf, Phyllis Sherlock, Carol Goodman, Martha Evans, Tricia LaFrance, Sally Smith, Deborah Sadowsky, Judith McGhee, Shanta Kamath, Jim McFerran, Tim Laue, and David H. Rosen.

Old pearl wrapped in silver, lies on the oak floor.
Dusty pearl, heart still beating, rests in my soul.

CHRIS PICHE

Climbing this life tree
a chance meeting you in the flesh
a ripe fruit plummets

CHRIS WHITE

Who stands in the way of
being here?
Its silhouette/shimmers and
thickens-

LINDA SHERMAN

I paint therefore I
am different than I was
I am in new terrain

PAUL HELMS

Morning love so sweet
What difference does it make?
Feet dance joy alive!

KAREN WICKHAM

October Demise Televised
BLACK MADONNA ASSASSINATED
White Millionaires Congress Cheers
Erica America Orphaned
Black Vet Dies Tomorrow

DALE O'BRIEN

Shadow's Dream

Self-contained alone
Hoping for welcome, waiting
Darkness holding light

DEAN SCHLECHT

Haiku in honor of documentary *Finding Vivian Maier*

Though unseen then she lives now
blooming while decayed
images of her gift here known

MARTHA BINSTADT

Cold, crisp, clear blue sky
Hummingbird finds food frozen
This side of glass warm

MARY MCDOUGAL

Softened Pain

Spirit comes to me,
Holds my hand,
Tells me lovingly
"I understand."

AVONELLE KLUESSENDORF

Mist in the mountains
Longer nights deepen dreaming
How will I find you?

PHYLLIS SHERLOCK

My love takes me by
surprise. A tree blooms in the
middle of winter.

CAROL GOODMAN

Mornings
Warm water soothes skin
Counting laps is a mantra
I swim: meditate.

MARTHA EVANS

At seven o'clock
Twelve geese descend on the green.
Family reunion.

TRICIA LAFRANCE

The Sun is gone.
How will the Darkness feed my soul?

SALLY SMITH
JIM KOCHER

Sitting in the sun
blue skies open my mind
peace and trust return

DEBORAH SADOWSKY

Sun shining through trees
Plants gold circles on our skin.
Pleased, I turn to you.
You are gone, gone many years.
This can't be. You were just here.

JUDITH MCGHEE

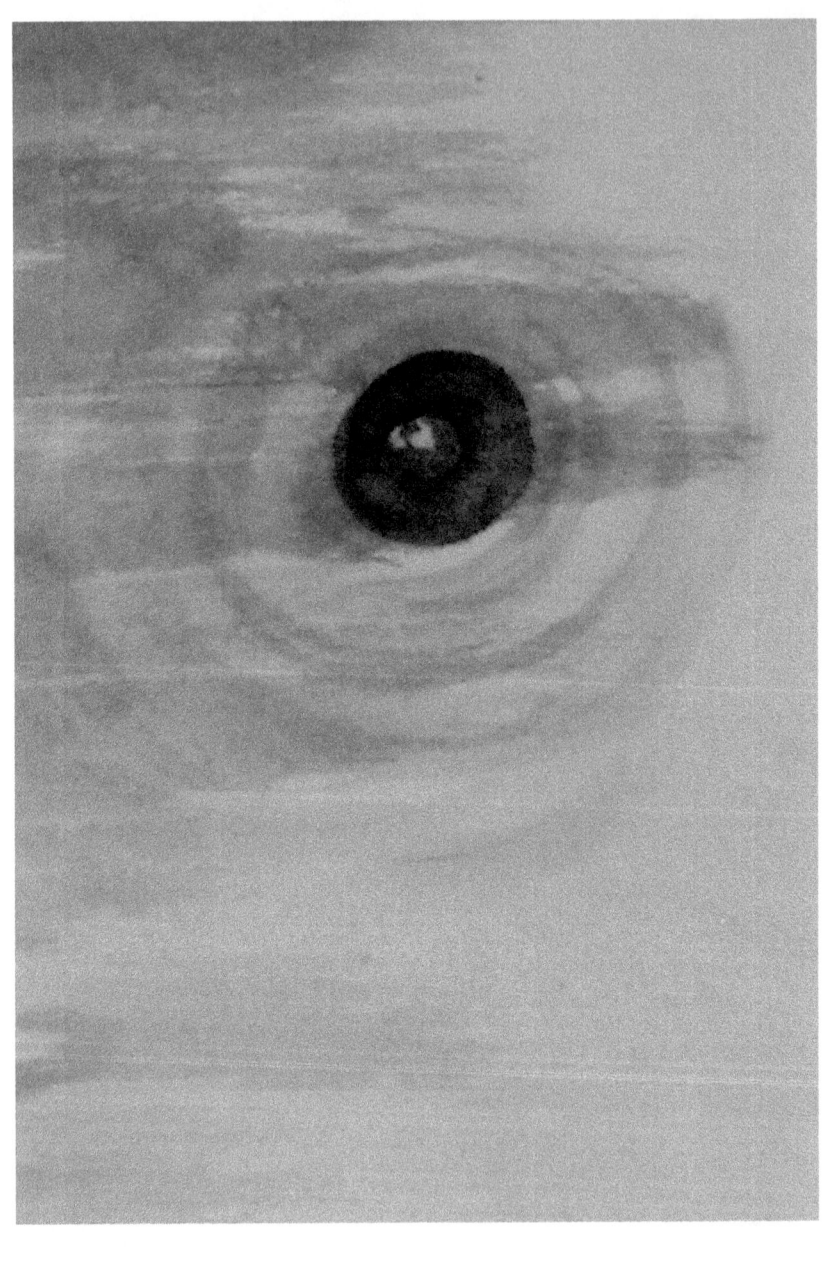

Raintime

Fall penumbras ring
Twinned in puddles, sing with rain
Brimming plainsong swells.

SHANTA KAMATH

apart from the others
looking out through the cold pane
for some sign of home

JIM MCFERRAN

where mists of dark dreams
reside too long in day's light
centers may not hold

TIM LAUE

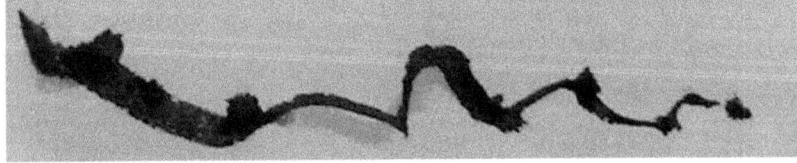

Slug trail on the porch . . .
Now, I understand my life.

DAVID H. ROSEN

(Previously published in *Your Daily Poem* May 21, 2014)

www.ingramcontent.com/pod-product-compliance
Lightning Source LLC
Chambersburg PA
CBHW061302040426
42444CB00010B/2476

INTO THE COURTYARD OF THE GENTILES

Reflections on Dominican Mission in the 21st Century

Lectures Delivered at the
75th Anniversary Assembly of the
Dominican Central Province

St. Dominic Priory, St. Louis, Missouri

January 2014

With an introduction by Donald Goergen, O.P

Charles E. Bouchard, O.P., Editor

NEW PRIORY PRESS
EXPLORING THE DOMINICAN VISION

Chicago 2015

Copyright © 2015
New Priory Press
Dominican Province of St. Albert the Great
1910 S. Ashland Avenue | Chicago, Illinois | 60608
www.newpriorypress.org

Table of Contents

Introduction 1
                          Donald J. Goergen, O.P.

Religious in the Church of the 21st Century............................ 7
                    Archbishop Joseph Tobin, C.Ss.R.

    Introduction 7
    The State of the Question: Three categories of lies 8
    Pope Benedict XVI..10
    A word from a friend 11
    What are we to do? We are his witnesses.................................14
    A Gospel based fraternity 17
    Mission on the margins and frontiers..21
    Conclusion..24

A Dominican Vision of Study: Into the Courtyard of the Gentiles...... 27
                    Michael Mascari, O.P.

Globalizing American Catholics [GACs]: The Continuing Relevance of the Dominican Vocation 37
                    Scott Appleby, Ph.D.

    Hope arising 38
    The World of the GACs 40
    Can the Dominicans Meet Their Part of the Challenge? 43